INVISIBLE STRINGS

BOOKS BY JIM MOORE

The New Body
What the Bird Sees
How We Missed Belgium (with Deborah Keenan)
The Freedom of History
The Long Experience of Love
Writing with Tagore
Minnesota Writes Anthology (co-editor)
Lightning at Dinner
Invisible Strings

INVISIBLE STRINGS

poems

Jim Moore

Graywolf Press

This publication is made possible by funding provided in part by a grant from the Minnesota State Arts Board, through an appropriation by the Minnesota State Legislature, a grant from the National Endowment for the Arts, and private funders. Significant support has also been provided by Target; the McKnight Foundation; and other generous contributions from foundations, corporations, and individuals. To these organizations and individuals we offer our heartfelt thanks.

Published by Graywolf Press
250 Third Avenue North, Suite 600
Minneapolis, Minnesota 55401

www.graywolfpress.org

Published in the United States of America
Printed in Canada

ISBN 978-1-55597-581-4

2 4 6 8 9 7 5 3 1
First Graywolf Printing, 2011

Library of Congress Control Number: 2010937519

Cover design: Kyle G. Hunter

Cover photos: JoAnn Verburg. *Thanksgiving* © 2000. Used with the permission of the photographer.

FOR JOANN

The black is beautiful,
but so, too, is the blue.

CONTENTS

ONLY EVERYWHERE

SPOLETO

SAINT PAUL

DISAPPEARING IN AMERICA

SAINT PAUL

SPOLETO

Nowhere is there place
to stop and live, so only
everywhere will do:
each and every grass-made hut soon leaves
its place within this withering world.

Saigyō

ONLY EVERYWHERE

LOVE IN THE RUINS

1

I remember my mother toward the end,

folding the tablecloth after dinner
    so carefully,
as if it were the flag
    of a country that no longer existed,
but once had ruled the world.

2

7 A.M. and the barefoot man

leaves his lover's house
    to go back to his basement room
across the alley. I nod hello,
    continuing to pick
the first small daffodils
    which just yesterday began to bloom.

3

Helicopter flies overhead

reminding me of that old war
    where one friend lost his life,
one his mind,
    and one came back happy
to be missing only an unnecessary finger.

4

I vow to write five poems today,

look down and see a crow
        rising into thick snow on 5th Avenue
as if pulled up by invisible strings,
        and already
there is only one to go.

5

Survived

another winter: my black stocking cap,
        my mismatched gloves,
my suspicious, chilly heart.

EPITAPH

He stole forsythia.
He lived for love.
He never got caught.

ALMOST SIXTY

1

     No, I don't know

the way to get there.
     Two empty suitcases sit in the corner,
if that's any kind of clue.

2

     This spring night,

everyone at the party
     younger than me
except for one man.
     We give each other the secret password.

3

     Tears? Of course, but also the marsh grass

near the Mississippi:
     your whispers and mine,
and the dog's long contented sighs.

ON THIS CLOUDY MAY DAY

I keep thinking
maybe June is what I need
to make me happy.

THOSE OTHERS

We lived at the end of an empire.

Sometimes we gathered in huge auditoriums
        and tried to understand.
Our shame did not save us,
        nor our sadness redeem us,
as we came to understand
        how others, far into the future,
would look back at us,
        shaking their heads: we hoped
in sorrow; more likely, anger.

FIVE CHARMS IN PRAISE OF BEWILDERMENT

1

    At first when you leave town,

the dog and I maintain dignified silence.
        After no more than two hours
I'm talking to her, after three
        she's telling me the story of her life.
I nod my head at every word,
        encouraging her
to take all the time she needs.

2

    I have the vice

of courting poems.
        Pathetic, I know.
I also like to watch *Oprah*
        if no one is around to notice.
That's right,
        I court poems, I watch *Oprah,*
I even let out wordless sighs late at night,
        and call them
my spring fields ploughed, my ready earth.

3

    Sitting quietly at dusk, I'll admit

my life goes like this:
        dark branches
scratching the still darker window.

4

"How are you?"

I ask a woman at work.
        "I have no idea,"
she replies,
        sounding pleased with herself
at the heartfeltness
        of her own bewilderment.

5

        We don't know,

can't possibly know,
        never have known,
never will know.
        We just don't know.

VIOLA,

absence courted by strings
in the night's first blue hour:
play me *that* song.

HOW WE GOT USED

The lousy passport photos were a start:

followed by the business
        with the coffee machine going *whoosh whoosh,*
then nothing.
        Your mother died, followed by mine.
After that,
        just attention to detail, plus touch.

THE TEMPEST: ACT 2 (SCENE 2 ENDS)

After "Lead the way,"

the stage door opens onto coolness.
        Actors stand outside
between scenes, smoking.
        Their faces are bruised with makeup
like plums newly ripened on a tree,
        the true sweetness showing through.

BIRTHDAY

1

Almost sixty:

from now on
    even begonias are amazing.

2

As in a dream

in which a light flashes
    and one has no choice
but to follow it,
    I ran after
the lightning bug
    along the railroad tracks
the night before my sixtieth birthday,
    a little drunk, unafraid,
laughing my fucking head off.

3

Only in dreams now

does my mother tell me
    to remember my sweater
on these cool summer evenings.

4

Walking past my two favorite pines,

still dripping from the rain,
       I point them out to you,
and you smile,
       and I am still sixty.

5

Cottonwoods in wind:

shakiness
       is the only way.

FIRST THE GOOD NEWS:

the girls still wrap blue scarves
      around their long necks,
then step out into the December air,
      laughing.

ALL THAT TALK OF THE MOON

1

When the woman across the way cries out at night

while making love,
        it is like the flash of lightning
that reawakens for a moment
        the ash
of all the fires
        that have previously burned us to the ground.

2

I love so badly

it amazes me
        you put the peony in my room.

3

Sometimes regret is simply all there is,

Saigyō,
        and all your talk of the moon
is only so much talk of the moon.

COLD GRAY OCTOBER SKY

I walk under it, head lowered, carrying four books I love.

IN THE LONG AFTERWARD

Almost 8 A.M., curtain drawn shut, lying in bed naked:

it's not the same as sex,
      but close
as a door slams,
      a shoe crunches on gravel,
walking away.
      Then the long afterward of lying still—
happy, lonely,
      who can say which—
the world
      just as it is, and the lover too,
just so.

SPOLETO

WAITING TO TAKE OFF

I try not to listen to the directions
     to the emergency exits,
how close they are,
     how very well lit.

AFTER DINNER

For many years, unable to speak the language,

I have sat silently at tables with Italians.
   Tonight, too. But this time I don't mind.
Joy enters the voices. Then sadness.
   We sit in moonlight, drink wine
until I understand every last word.

   After dinner, you and I do the walk
around the old fortress where power
   had once seemed the point of things.
The sound of crickets and a samba band, faintly,
   from the Communist Party
party, far down the hill. Our dog
   seems to lead the way, but really,
everything leads everything else
   around the abandoned fortress.

MIDNIGHT AND THE LOW SOUND OF WATER

from a stone fountain. His dog suddenly barking at us,
    an old man, vocal chords gone,
puts his hand to his throat, whispers through his voice box,
    Tomorrow
he will be your friend for life.

ANGELS

Inside the dark church

Perugino's angels
    hurtle through the air:
great unreachable joy,
    while outside,
one workman on his knees
    slowly taps a huge stone
back into place
    in front of the store
where all the shoes are on sale.

TUESDAY

Some days, I am capable

only of caring about my new chestnut-colored shoes
    with the red laces, which in Italy
seem demure, but in Minnesota
    will give off the faint whiff
of a clown gone overboard, drowning
    in his own ridiculous sea.

FRIDAY

The young Americans arrive,

backpacks and loud voices,
    such excitement
at being Elsewhere. "I miss my mother,"
    I hear one say to another,
standing at a railing from which you can see
    darkness coming from miles away
across the valley, the same darkness
    you will be given to call your own
after your own mother is gone.

SATURDAY

In the café yesterday,

the one that looks out on the ruins
    of the old amphitheater,
I was in the middle of reading
    yet another poem about death
when I looked up. A man was standing there
    hand open, silently hoping
I might give.

He stared straight at me,
the brown skin of his palm like a blind eye
    looking out at nothing.
I shook my head no
    and went back to my book, death
returning to death.

BLOOD IN OUR HEADLIGHTS, CAR WRECKED, THE BOAR DEAD

Out of the darkness, men come
     with knives. They work quickly,
muttering back and forth.
     By the time the police arrive,
the boar is gone. The foreigners,
     each one of us, stand around
the wrecked car,
     everyone still alive.

     And then

the moment becomes a story,
     cut open as completely as the boar had been,
all of us making use of it
     in whatever ways we need
until our lives and the names
     we were given never to let go of
go.
     And even laughter and even our fears:
gone,
     along with the boar and our bewilderment,
traceless now inside the unending sound
     of crickets, the brown dust
soaked in blood.

SLEEPING WITH *MONA LISA*

The young woman on the train

uses as a bookmark
    a postcard of the *Mona Lisa*.
She sleeps, while in the distant field
    at the edge of the painting
just poking up through her book
    I see the light da Vinci loved,
the blue light of ambulances at night
    when they pulse out their warnings.

TRIUMPHS

The triumphs in his life
were so quiet, he should be ashamed.
That she would touch his back
on the correct place
at dawn.
That when it came to swallows
near dusk he acknowledged
no peer.
Happiness was never a thing
he could claim as a specialty.
But sitting by the window
in the middle of an endless winter night,
now that is a thing
he can do. Decorum
under a black sky, patience
in moonlight, dozing, then waking again.
That the sight of the dog sleeping mattered
was a triumph
not just anyone
could understand. Or the thought
of sleep itself and its rose
pillowcase, or leaving it behind
at 4 A.M., sitting
at that dark window,
wide awake for no reason,
letting himself get distracted again
by the ruined garden
where the neighbor lives
who rarely bothers to speak
now that her son has died.
She likes to stand by her wrinkled poppies
early in the morning,
when she thinks she is alone.
But she is not alone. *Triumph*

was always the wrong word,
wasn't it? No,
        not triumph, but something much closer,
like the remaining leaves on October trees,
        all glory and dissolution.

SAINT PAUL

TRYING TO LEAVE SAINT PAUL

1

Little streets of Saint Paul

that lead nowhere. One of them
    ends where quiet drunks sit
in the old September grass
    on top of a hill.
Street cars used to run here,
    through a tunnel cut into the hill.
The sun rides so low
    in the cloud-filled western sky,
it makes the empty bottles glow.

2

How far away

it is possible to go from Saint Paul
    in a single night of raucous dreams:
I wake up before dawn,
    joyful, moon sliding in
through the slats
    of our broken bamboo curtain.

3

A boy and his father

cross the street. The first depends
    on the second. The second
fumbles for a map.

4

      Yesterday we almost did it,

took off from Saint Paul,
      driving south thirty hours
to Florida, almost gave in
      to sunlight, warmth, the sea.
The biopsy report had come back negative,
      making me greedy for more:
coconuts, fresh shrimp, crickets
      past midnight under a full moon.
I did so want
      to begin driving
and never stop.

THE FOUR STAGES OF LOVE

1

    My father: how he lifted

his glass at our wedding,
    and with shaking hand
welcomed love into my life.

2

    Getting out of bed,

you run the bath water
    and I sleep a moment longer,
dreaming of a Greek island
    and flowers in a deep cavern.
Very slowly I climb down
    for a closer look.

3

    Driving the December road to Saint Paul

in winter sunlight,
    Bill Evans on the radio. Maybe
this is actually paradise,
    you said, and on we went
from there.

4

I want to believe it

when the pine tree out my window
        tells me I don't have to be afraid
for my own death, not even,
        Love, for yours.

ABOVE ALL, DON'T FORGET

that empty lacrosse field at dawn,
    the brown grass of December,
the solitary runner jogging past
    under the three pine trees
you see each morning first thing,
    even before you remember
to worry about what you do deserve,
    what you don't.

INSTEAD OF CALM

1

An old man reads the newspaper

with complete focus, such a peaceful face,
    and that checked, immaculate cap.
Slowly his fingers move down each column,
    line by line.
Nothing is missed, not one single scandal
    or horrific accident.
God forbid I ever become so calm.
    Head bowed, he sees it all,
never smiling or frowning.

2

After your cousin's death—

sudden, accidental at eighteen—your father
    told me you went for a long run
along the edge of a golf course, then around
    a small pond. You ended
coming up the hill to your house
    at the very place you began.
You were still breathing deeply,
    regularly, and there was nothing
to be done for it.

CELL PHONE

When their marriage ends

the two friends must be called,
first one, then the other.

OF ALL PLACES

1

      After the death

of our young friend's brother,
      she looks at me differently,
almost with suspicion,
      as if there was something about this life
I had deliberately not told her.

2

      That all calm is a false calm

I keep learning again and again.
      And yet,
the sound of water falling on stone
      early one warm June morning,
in this world of all places.

3

      Her friends come now

every day since the death of her brother
      to walk the floor along with her
as she sweeps up
      in the little café
where we came to know her
      before the grief of her true life began.

POEM WITHOUT AN ENDING

Listening to acorns fall
such a lovely sound
    I thought it was the whole poem
until I saw the girl in the paper
    with the mussed hair
the bombed bus
    no one bothering yet
to close those two black eyes

MOONLIGHT SHINING BARELY

1

      When the drunk woman approached us

wanting only one dollar—something to do with Lent
      and a flat tire—
we gave it to her. It was a cold February night,
      raining. Afterward, she put the cross
across her own forehead with her own fingers
      as if she were both priest and penitent,
and we were the rest of the congregation,
      waiting patiently in line
both to forgive and be forgiven.

2

      One car moving slowly

at 5 A.M. on a dirt road
      across the river and then, suddenly,
this whole life is gone.

3

      The more I study it now,

the art of my superiors, the more
      I see how it is mostly darkness.
Though sometimes at the edge
      of a canvas

a bit of moonlight shines barely
     on women mourning
a dead Christ, their faces ravaged
     by a kindness
unknown to me.

HER JOY

She lines up a chair at her window,

sets a book next to the chair:
        everything waits for everything else
to catch up. At ninety,
        reading Proust in French,
still looking out the window.
        It all matters:
the postman with the well-trimmed beard
        who lives across the street,
his regular route;
        how each night
the sun sets and still the world goes on,
        even into darkness.

NOT KNOWING HOW TO SAY GOOD-BYE

On the last night of winter,

seven old friends
    staying late at the party,
unwilling to call it a night.

DISAPPEARING IN AMERICA

HOMEFRONT

1

    Here at home

nothing changes. Middle-aged men
     send young men to war.
Old men wake up before dawn
     waiting for the light to come
as they gaze from a window
     at oak trees
arriving without haste out of the darkness,
     tears in our eyes,
not that they help.

2

    "Maybe I should go to the Civil War cemetery and write a poem,"

I say. "Sounds like a really bad poem," you say.
     I sit in the lobby of the Hampton Inn instead
and watch TV images from Thailand,
     where the living hang on to palm trees
just above the raging flood
     for as long as they can.

IN THE SHADOW OF THE ROD AND REEL CLUB

1

Chilly morning at the sea: I see

jade-green water, the turquoise blue, eternity
        everywhere I look. But what really gets me
is the shape of your skirt on a hanger,
        hooked on the showerhead.

2

A single pelican flies by

with the feel about it
        of an ancient culture.
No one speaks that language anymore.

3

At the town harbor for the last time,

no doubt I will forget
        the way the black dog
on the wet sand chases the red ball
        until the end of time.

4

On the same day

the bomb goes off in Baghdad,
        I watch a green palm tree

climb easily into gray sky,
      rain whispering all down
its knotty, stubborn spine.

      A wedding party dies.
The parents and the bride,
      the photographer
hidden in the wings,
      and the children
not yet conceived, also
      hidden in the wings.

5

      Sitting by the sea, waiting for darkness:

after all, I've come this far.

6

      Too bad. It's time to go,

but the fishermen will stay behind,
      working the shadows
in back of the Rod and Reel Club:
      steady now; be patient; just a little longer.

THANKSGIVING

1

The wet wood costs us real money,

but these dry chips he threw in for free.
It's no way to run a business,
but our fire burns beautifully.

2

On Thanksgiving, the phone

suddenly stops working. For this, too,
Lord, we give thanks.

3

Giant pines in November sunlight:

sitting inside their shadows
what is death to me?

4

Everyone is always younger than me

and more beautiful. Actually,
this arrangement works.

5

Three black dogs in gray light

at dusk, tails up, faces together:
    nothing is missing.

IF I COULD HAVE BEEN A BUDDHIST,

I would have accepted humbly,
    without judgment, the world
as it was given:
    the whisper
of my sister's voice on the phone,
    telling me of her friend's murder.

Instead,
    I love what I can:
your black hair on the white pillow,
    the sound of a crow calling out,
even as it grows more distant.

NEBRASKA FRAGMENTS

1

     The unmoving shadows

of black-and-white cows,
     a river's blue vein.
Then sunlight
     flooding down on the confused hearts of those
going east on 80, those going west.

2

     How many more years

will it go like this:
     cheap motel room outside Omaha,
a glimpse of the yellow ball
     under a desk,
the dog just too sleepy to fool with it?

DISAPPEARING IN AMERICA

1

      At a coffee stand

in front of a World War I memorial
        near the school where I teach,
a young woman
        dispenses the sweet with the bitter.
People line up
      to pay her for it.

2

      Will this be the day

when I stop
        on the way home from work,
even for a moment,
        at Hennepin and Lake
and bow my head?
        Do you know
the corner I mean,
        where they planted that little elm
which never quite took root?

3

      It is difficult to call it my own,

but impossible not to,
        this world
in which a boy,

both legs shattered by a land mine,
then flown to New York,
    smiles from his bed
at the doctor who amputated them
    cleanly, just above the knees.

4

    My single star is gone, the one

I like to call mine. Instead, a thick haze
    of moonlight. Just as my mother did
when she was growing old, I sit in the darkness,
    getting used to how little I can see.

LAST NIGHT I DREAMED THAT MAN, THE ONE

from the photos on a leash.
     His slight moan
has nothing to do with sex, his fear
     is not a thing I know
what to do with, and yet,
     here we are in the same dream,
each of us ashamed
     that the other exists.

WHEN ALL ELSE FAILS

1

You make me laugh,

then I make you laugh, and so
it goes, this last day of fall.

2

Those two, newly in love,

standing in a bookstore
near the back:
for them, holding the same book,
while helping each other
turn its pages,
is enough.

3

The setting moon and the night

move silently in opposite directions,
old friends
no longer needing to bother with words.

4

Last fall crickets: impossible

not to write
one more poem.

SAINT PAUL

THERE GOES THAT LITTLE MUTT
FROM DOWN THE STREET

and the man, his owner,
     walking together in the cold
December darkness:
     love takes you
where you need to go,
     no exceptions.

ANNIVERSARY

1

      Reading the poet on Nothingness,

I suppose it is a higher calling than love.
      And yet, love
is what I have been given,
      not Nothingness.
Who am I to argue
      with the lesser fate:
twenty-five years tomorrow.

2

      Squandered so much:

but most of all
      those long silences together,
sometimes at noon over lunch, sometimes
      very late at night
after a long day working, those
      we squandered most beautifully of all.

3

      One bird, then another

begins to sing
      outside the store
where you try on dresses.
      The black is beautiful,
but so, too, is the blue.

EXAMPLES

The pale green walls of the little room

we've been given to use.
    Or another example:
the calm way a siren sounds
    after six inches of snow.
Winter light, for sure,
    as the sound of your foot on the stair
grows fainter.

NOT TAKING IT PERSONALLY

1 (Thesis)

We go to the same café

as the twelve-step coffee drinkers.
A new one today: young, shaky,
purple hair. Already, she smiles well.
The hair will go soon,
the smudged look in her eyes will
slowly drain away.
I've seen it all before:
what happens, mother,
when they do finally stop.

2 (Antithesis)

In the room where the friends meet,

the thirteen-year-old boy sprawls.
While the grown-ups talk,
he eats three Reese's Peanut Butter Cups
in search of just the right amount
of sweetness. Only then,
does he let himself fall asleep
as we go on worrying aloud
about the world.
We stare at him as we speak,
as those who are lonely
will stare into a fire late at night,
the world as we wish it were.

3 (Synthesis)

Each song on the CD

more sad than the one before.
I need to remember
I'm not the first, won't be the last.

MY FAME

Don't think I didn't want it.

But moonlight distracted me. Even dust
     in sunlight in summer
distracted. Both
     were my friends, knew me
for who I was,
     forgave me everything.

BLIZZARD

DAY 1

      As snow begins to fall,

a cement mixer slowly turns, so patiently,
      across the street under bare January branches.
How I wish I were the man I'm not.

DAY 2

      Snow blocks the bridge.

No one can cross.
      How sad life is,
how calm.

DAY 3

      My beard grows white.

I could say like waves or like snow;
      but really,
white like an old man's beard.

HER BITTERNESS MAKES SENSE—

old, blind, affronted—but still
      I would hope for her
this short April dusk,
      as yet unspoken for.

TRUE ENOUGH,

I have forgotten many things.
But I do remember
    the bank of clover along the freeway
we were passing thirty years ago
    when someone I loved made clear to me
it was over.

AFTERWARD

At age seventy, in winter,

Corot paints a pond in gray light
        and a girl kneeling before it, face half turned
toward the old man painting.
        A gray birch rises beside her,
slightly bent, blackened
        around the edges.
I sit on a bench by a real pond
        in a small museum,
every so often
        lowering my eyes,
as if the painting might need
        a moment of privacy
in this public room:

        as in a hospital, near the end,
when a solitary death
        becomes the work of all involved,
mother and son and daughter, father
        going away. Afterward,
I sneaked outside
        and walked in a scruffy park
where two girls swung under giant elms.
        The new day began
and I felt like an old man myself,
        standing before my own gray pond
in shining light.
        I watched the two girls,
life in its great rising arcs swinging
        toward death, and death
flies away. Pick up your brush,
        old man.
Do not be afraid.

PIGEONS IN A BLACK SKY,

flying straight into the rain
      on white wings, moving far away
from the very idea of day and night
      into pure storm, never once
looking back, the way they say
      the dying don't,
once it is clear
      that this world
is such a small beginning.

ON THE DAY AFTER

The old woman who lives across the street

runs her vacuum
        on the day after Christmas,
cleaning up after the silence
        of the day before.
Two small geraniums in the window
        lean into one another
like people whispering at a funeral:
        signs of life.

GRADUALLY, THAT HALF-SMILE

my father so often wore as he got older
    takes me on as a project.

AFTER LIFE

1

      In her last days

my aunt marveled at how kind everyone was.
      All they wanted of her
was that she swallow her pills.
      They even broke them in half.
Still, she couldn't do it.
      She had just enough energy left
to be moved by kindness; not a bit more.

2

      It's not anything

you can take with you
      into the next world,
this dawn.

3

      Who would have thought,

sunlight, tugboat's
      thick black smoke, this slow river,
who would have thought
      nothing ends?

4

    I decide not to bother

putting a new battery in the clock:
    7 A.M. for good now, new light in the trees
and a small wind that will go on forever.

SPOLETO

MY SWALLOWS AGAIN

Early morning: cuckoos and swallows crying out as if it's the first time ever.

The sound of hammers.

The way sunlight looks on the Scotch broom growing on the side of the hill across the valley from our window: even after all these years I keep thinking I'll find the right words to say it all.

I don't sleep much, but this tiredness helps me see the man by the side of the road, holding a heavy bag of groceries and waiting for the bus while he leans against a light pole, eyes closed.

Staring at the cloudy sky, I try to act as if this sadness is just what I need.

It was only this one time we lived, you in your black T-shirt, standing next to an olive tree, sun shining down, and me frowning a little so I could see you all the more clearly.

Isn't there some way to finish this life sitting at an open window on a rainy day listening to birds call out?

Inside of life, inside of death, swallows keep flying.

A small deer runs across my path and suddenly I am no longer lonely.

My swallows again. And yet, I couldn't stop myself thinking about what would happen should you go first.

Olive trees about the size of people; so quiet near dusk, their silver leaves. And their way of not minding my troubled thoughts.

If my parents had graves, it's on a warm cloudy day like this I would go to visit them.

Stupid teenage boys grin their stupid grins and honk their horn at you while you stand motionless under your dark cloth. Thank God I was never sixteen.

Saw that old man again today, the one who looks down at each step he takes, as if needing to convince himself that there is somewhere else he needs to go.

Rain every day for two weeks, wet olive trees, wet poppies, you under an umbrella, laughing.

First they tear up the old sidewalk, then put in the new one. I hope they understand how short life is.

The swallows are leaving; maybe going away is a thing I too can do with a little flourish and swoop at the end.

The old man in suit and tie sits on the park bench, leans forward in his elegant way so he won't miss a word of what the girl with the tattoo is trying to explain to him. Even at this distance I can see he doesn't have a clue, his happiness as complete as his confusion.

A woman feeds her sister's cat each morning while the sister is gone. *Amore, amore,* she calls and the cat comes. I sit in the shadows, my death nearby, neither of us minding the presence of the other.

My friend's hands tremble from his illness as he makes the ice cream using fresh melon, then spots it with a touch of some dark liqueur.

It may be that dying is a little like leaving Spoleto: all this confusion and worry about catching a train that is only going to Perugia.

Seagulls crying out in the piazza. What are they doing here so far from the sea?

How can you not love a country where the meter maids wear high heels?

On the other side of the mountain, where I cannot see, I'm sure another old man must sit, just as I do now, like this on a couch in his bathrobe, lonely and happy.

ACKNOWLEDGMENTS

Many of these poems have appeared in various configurations and sequences in the following publications: *Flurry, Lightning at Dinner* (Graywolf Press, 2005), *Low Down and Coming On: A Feast of Delicious and Dangerous Poems about Pigs* (edited by James P. Lenfestey, Red Dragonfly Press, 2010), the *New Yorker, Noon,* the *Paris Review, Pirene's Fountain, Pleiades, Prairie Schooner,* the *Rake, Saint Paul Almanac, Sleet,* and *Water~Stone Review.*

"Blizzard" was published as a broadside by The Colorado College.

The book was a pleasure to write but a challenge to edit. The following people helped tremendously: Michael Dennis Browne, Jane Hilberry, Jane Hirshfield, Tony Hoagland, Deborah Keenan, Patricia Kirkpatrick, Dave Mason, Gail Mazur, Fiona McCrae, Carol Moldaw, Alice Quinn, Jeff Shotts, Arthur Sze, Carol Venezia, Michael Venezia, JoAnn Verburg, and J. P. White.

The epigraph by Saigyō appears in *Awesome Nightfall: The Life, Times, and Poetry of Saigyō,* edited and translated by William R. LaFleur, published by Wisdom Publications, Boston, 2003.

JIM MOORE is the author of six previous collections of poetry, including *Lightning at Dinner*. His poems have appeared in *American Poetry Review*, the *Nation*, the *New Yorker*, the *Paris Review*, the *Threepenny Review*, and in many other magazines and anthologies. Moore has received numerous awards and fellowships from the Bush Foundation, The Loft, the McKnight Foundation, and the Minnesota State Arts Board. He teaches at Hamline University in Saint Paul, Minnesota, and at The Colorado College in Colorado Springs, as well as online through the University of Minnesota Split Rock Arts Program. He is married to the photographer JoAnn Verburg. They live in Saint Paul, Minnesota, and Spoleto, Italy.

Design and composition by BookMobile Design and
Publishing Services, Minneapolis, Minnesota. Manufactured
by Transcontinental on acid-free 100 percent
postconsumer wastepaper.